To Abby, Jack, Henry, and Charlie,
who ask me all the best questions.
—D.M.

Published by Yeehoo Press
6540 Lusk Blvd, Ste C152, San Diego, CA 92121
www.yeehoopress.com

The illustrations for this book were created in Photoshop.
Edited by Molly Yao Shen
Designed by Si Ye
Supervised by Luyang Xue

Library of Congress Control Number:2022943124
ISBN: 978-1-953458-47-6
Printed in China First Edition
1 2 3 4 5 6 7 8 9 10

Lights On!

Glow-in-the-Dark
Deep Ocean Creatures

Written by Donna B. McKinney

Illustrated by Daniella Ferretti

YEEHOO
PRESS

Near the ocean's surface,
the first rays of sunrise bathe the waters.
Here fish, seals, and turtles
swim, splash, and eat in a world lit by sunlight.

But farther below,
in the deeper waters
below the sunlight zone,
the water world dims,
gradually growing
darker, darker, darker.
Lights out!

Deep in the ocean,
where sunlight cannot reach,
it's so dark
and always night.
What can be seen in this dark,
deep ocean world?

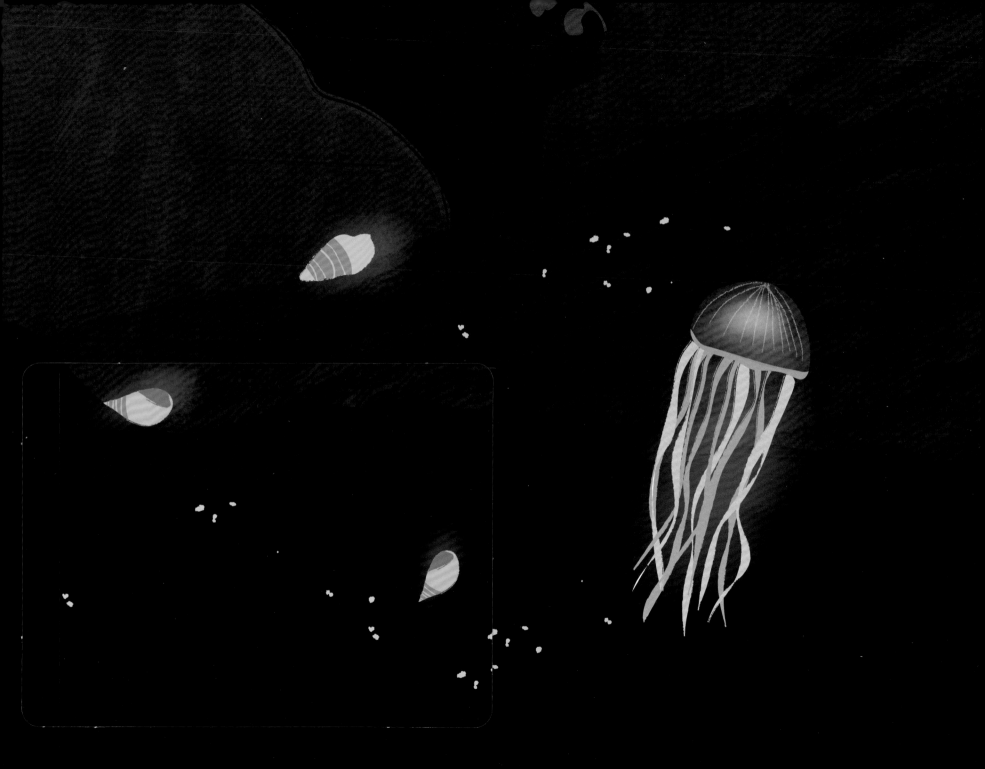

On the water's surface,
morning sunshine flashes on the waves.

But farther below,
under the sunlight zone,
waters where no sunshine reaches,
the lanternfish carries its own tiny lights.

Every night it swims up, up, up,
toward warmer waters
where food can be found.

When daylight returns to those waters,
the lanternfish swims down, down, down,
where midnight darkness hides it again.

On the water's surface,
the glowing sun climbs higher in the sky.

But farther below, deep in the ocean,
where darkness abounds, the vampire squid
moves in midnight-dark waters.

Swoosh, swoosh!

The vampire squid glides, its giant eyes
watchful in its dark, dark world.
If predators swim too close, it squirts
clusters of twinkling lights from its
tentacles.

Flap, flap, flap.

The vampire squid moves its fins like a
bird in flight and swooshes away to safety.

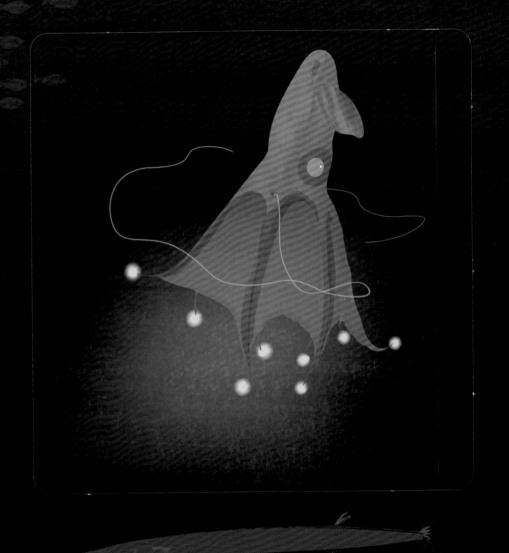

On the water's surface, the sun starts its
slow slide into the afternoon.
But farther below, in the midnight waters
where no sunlight reaches,
the pocket shark glows.

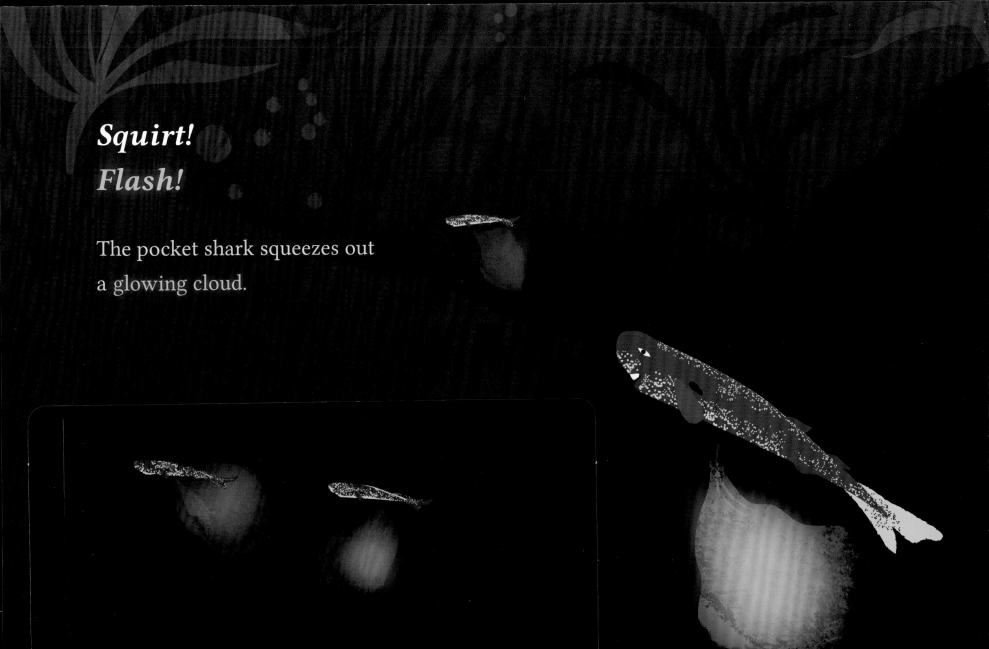

Squirt!
Flash!

The pocket shark squeezes out
a glowing cloud.

On the water's surface,

the dusky haze between daylight and darkness descends.

But farther below, in the waters where sunlight cannot reach,

the tiny fireworm moves about.

As the sun sets and before the
moon rises, female fireworms
swim upward from the seafloor,
their bodies casting a glowing light.

They swim in tight circles,
searching for a mate.
Drawn by the spinning circles of
light, male fireworms swim near.

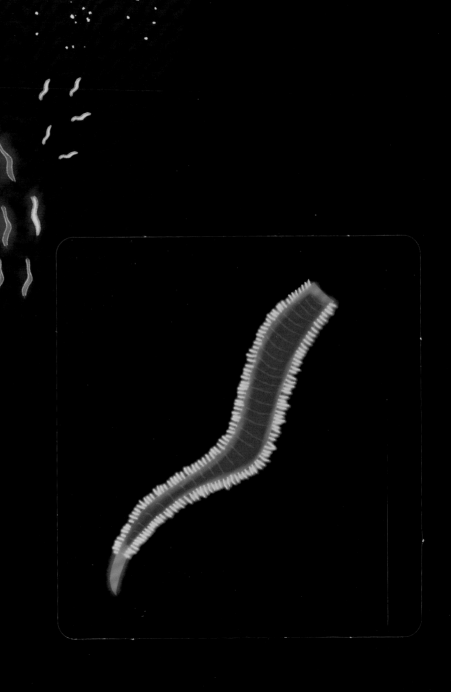

On the water's surface,
the orange glowing sun slips below the horizon.

But farther below,
in the deep down, dark waters
where no daylight can be found,
the viperfish prowls for dinner.

The viperfish's light looks like
a fishing pole strapped to its back,
with a tiny light bulb at the very end.

Blink! Blink! Blink!

Attracted by the strange glow of light,
smaller fish swim closer and closer.
With its large mouth and needle-sharp fangs,
the viperfish munches its meal.

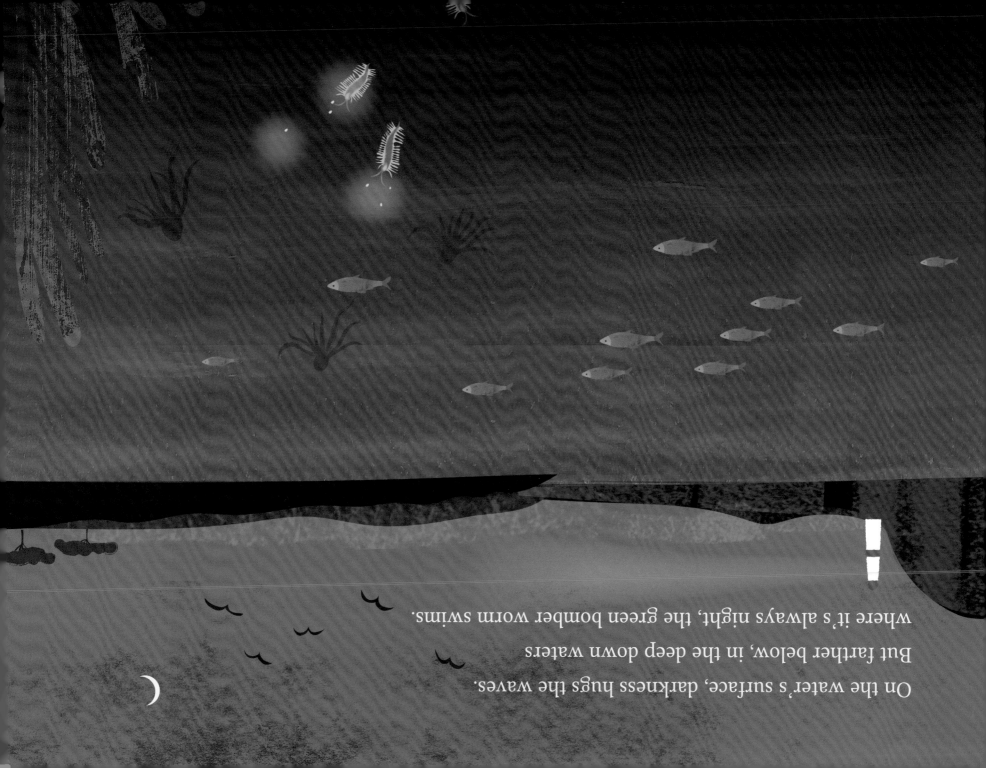

On the water's surface, darkness hugs the waves.

But farther below, in the deep down waters

where it's always night, the green bomber worm swims.

Using its long bristles as tiny paddles,
the green bomber worm swims skillfully.
But when a dangerous predator comes
too near, the green bomber worm
releases tiny balls of green color from
its body as a distraction.
With the predator dazzled by the lights,
green bomber worm paddles to safety.

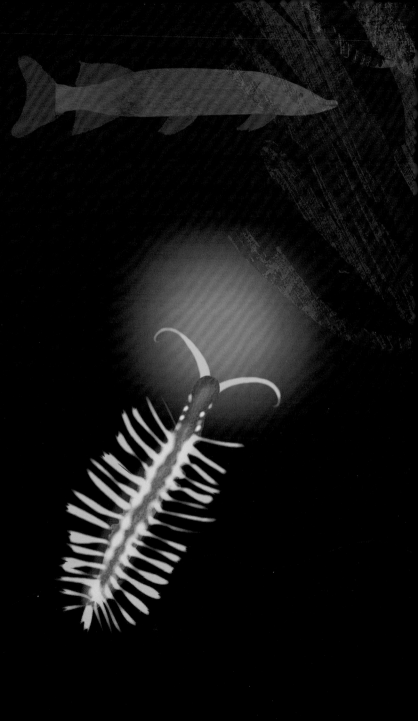
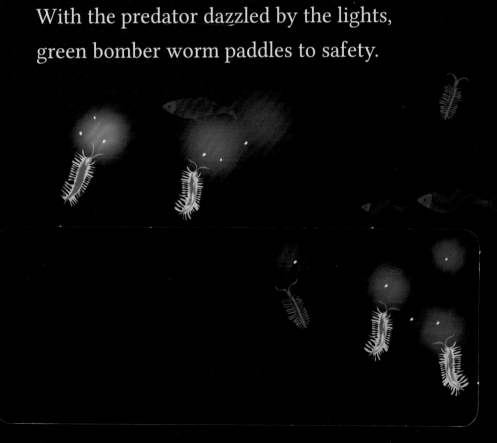

At the ocean's surface, all is darkness.

But farther below, in the
deep
down,
dark waters
where night darkness
covers everything,
there is light to be found . . .

Creatures seek mates.

Creatures search for a meal.

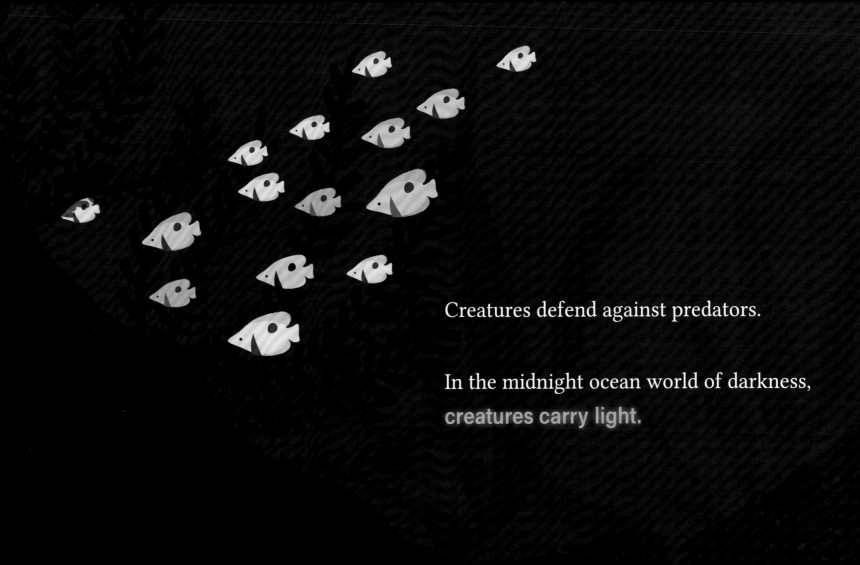

Creatures defend against predators.

In the midnight ocean world of darkness,
creatures carry light.

Bioluminescence Abounds in the Ocean Waters

About 76% of ocean creatures, including fish, worms, sea stars, and jellyfish, use a superpower: bioluminescence.
It is a chemical reaction that takes place inside a living creature and creates light.

Like the Flame of Small Candles

It is likely that Christopher Columbus and his crew saw fireworms on October 11, 1492 as their ship sailed near San Salvador island. Columbus wrote in his diary that he saw "the flame of a small candle alternately raised and lowered" in the waters.

Bioluminescence Leads the Way Home

Pilots have used bioluminescence to guide them to safety at night. In 1954, fighter pilot James Lovell was flying near the coast of Japan when his plane's instruments stopped working. He had no way to guide the plane to safety! But he spied a green streak in the water below him and realized it was bioluminescence from dinoflagellates in a ship's wake. He followed the trail of eerie, glowing light in the waters back to a safe landing spot.

Questions Remain

Scientists are still searching for answers about glow-in-the-dark creatures. They ask questions like:
What happens inside a creature's body that makes it glow in the dark?
Why are there so many glow-in-the-dark creatures in the ocean, but not on land?
How can glow-in-the-dark creatures help us better understand the oceans?

We still have much to learn about these mysterious creatures who live in the deepest waters. Maybe one day you will find answers to these questions.